GUIDE TO AIRLINERS

Andrew Kershaw

Illustrated by Cliff and Wendy Meadway

Designed by Jane Olliver

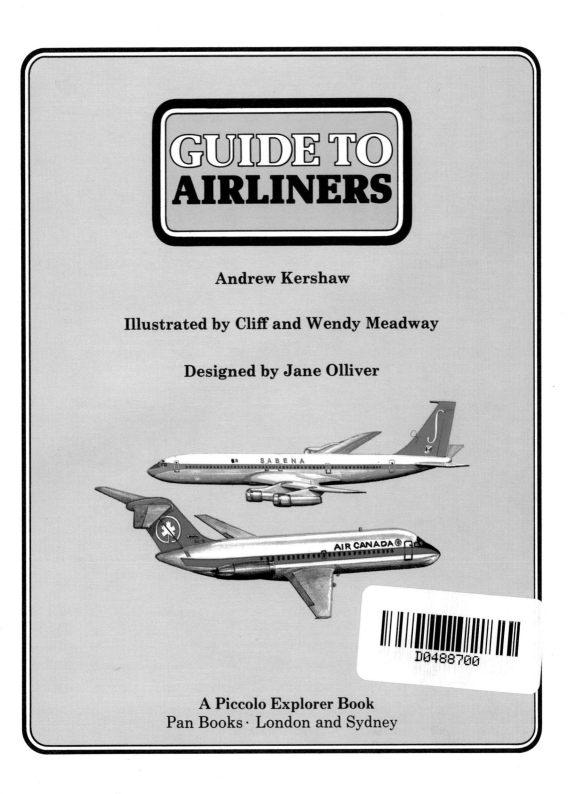

A Piccolo Explorer Book

Pan Books · London and Sydney

Below, clockwise left to right:
Lockheed Vega, Comet 4B,
Boeing 247, Caravelle and
McDonnell Douglas DC-10.

Contents

About This Book

Flying in a modern jet airliner is an exciting way to travel. From eight kilometres up, moving at 16 kilometres a minute, rivers seem to curve like fine pencil lines, pin-head icebergs sparkle and clouds look like cotton-wool mountains against the blue sky.

This book is packed with information about airliners that operate today, airlines and airports. The history of air travel is also covered, and many of the best-known airliners of the past are described and shown in pictures. Most important of all, this guide book will help the young reader to identify different airliners that are in service around the world today.

What to Look For

Apart from all the romance of flying – the roar of the engines, travel to faraway places, and the excited crowds at airports – the actual airliners themselves are quite amazing. Many weigh hundreds of tonnes and yet they can cruise smoothly along, eight to nine kilometres over the Earth, at around 1000 km/h. Types like the Boeing 747s may carry as many as 500 people, while Concorde, for example, only has room for about 140 passengers. But Concorde flies more than twice as fast as the Boeing 747 'jumbo'.

Although at first sight all airliners might look very similar, there are really several different

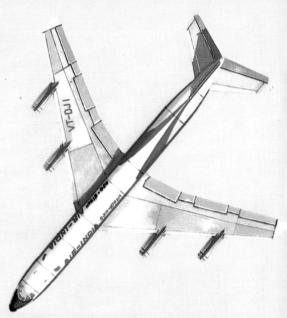

▲ Swept-back wings These are found on almost all fast-flying jet airliners and warplanes. They help with lift and streamlining and come between straight and delta wings.

▼ Straight wings This wing-shape gives the most lift, and it is usually found on old aircraft built before swept wings arrived in the 1950s, or on slow or light aircraft.

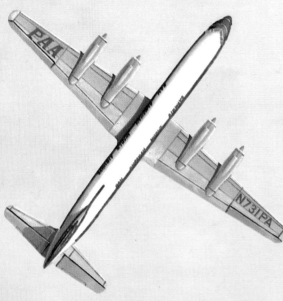

types of designs. The main variations are in the number of engines and their positioning (two, three or four; below the wings or at the back). The shape of the wings also differs (straight, swept-back or delta) and the tails are of many different designs.

With practice, by looking for these features it becomes quite easy to identify different makes of planes. Then, when you know the type of airliner, it is possible to find out how fast and how far it can fly, how many passengers it carries, when it was built and so on. By knowing an airliner's range (short, medium or long) it is even possible to guess roughly how far it is going or has come.

Tail Assemblies

An aircraft's tailfin keeps it going in a steady direction; the rudder turns it left or right; and tailplanes keep it level, when diving or climbing.

Triple vertical tailplane

TWA

Low-mounted tailplane

T-shaped tailplane

High-mounted tailplane

JAT

▼ **Delta wings** Really fast flight does not need wings. Instead, like an arrow-head, streamlined delta-shaped fins are enough to give stability. (Δ is the Greek letter 'delta'.)

F-WTBA

Engine Arrangements

Wingspan 44·84 m

▲ **Airbus A300B** This new short-range airliner has a *turbofan* under each wing.

Wingspan 34·30 m

▲ **Caravelle** A rear-engined, twin-jet French airliner which appeared in 1959.

Wingspan 39·87 m

▲ **DC-10** This big 1971 'airbus' has an engine under each wing and one high in the tailfin.

Wingspan 32·92 m

▲ **Boeing 727** The world's most successful airliner, it has three rear-mounted turbofans.

Wingspan 59·64 m

▲ **Boeing 747** The four-engined 'jumbo' is unmistakable with its big bubbled fuselage.

Wingspan 44·55 m

▲ **Super VC-10** With a high tail and four engines at the back, this is a classic of the 1960s.

5

Inside an Airliner

It takes many years to design a new airliner that is fast, quiet, comfortable, safe and cheap to run. First, knowing what the airline company needs, the chief designer draws up a general plan of the new plane. He or she has to decide how many engines it needs, its size, the best wing shape and so on.

Nowadays many big airliners – like the TriStar, Super VC-10 and DC-10 – are built with engines mounted at the back. This makes take-offs easier and is quieter for the passengers. But underwing engines, which need stronger wings, are easier to repair or replace.

Once the basic decisions are made an army of workers starts to design and test the whole aircraft down to the last rivet and seat cushion. Factories around the world often build different sections, which are then assembled into the *prototype*. Eventually, after more tests on the ground and in the air, the new airliner will be ready to go into production.

▼ **Boeing 747** This airliner can carry up to 490 passengers. But the basic passenger model shown here usually carries only 374 people. The spacious cabins provide plenty of room for all the passengers.

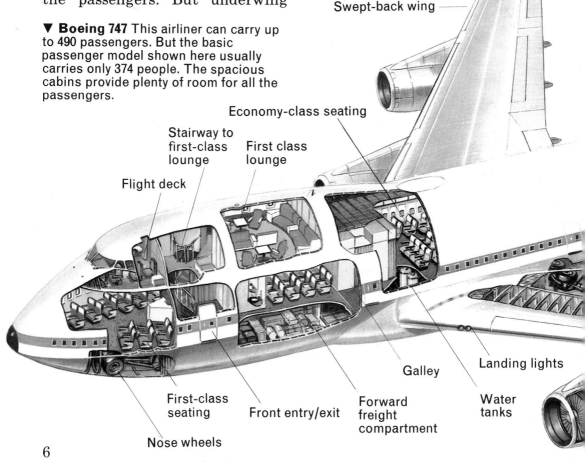

Swept-back wing

Economy-class seating

Stairway to first-class lounge

First class lounge

Flight deck

First-class seating

Front entry/exit

Forward freight compartment

Galley

Landing lights

Water tanks

Nose wheels

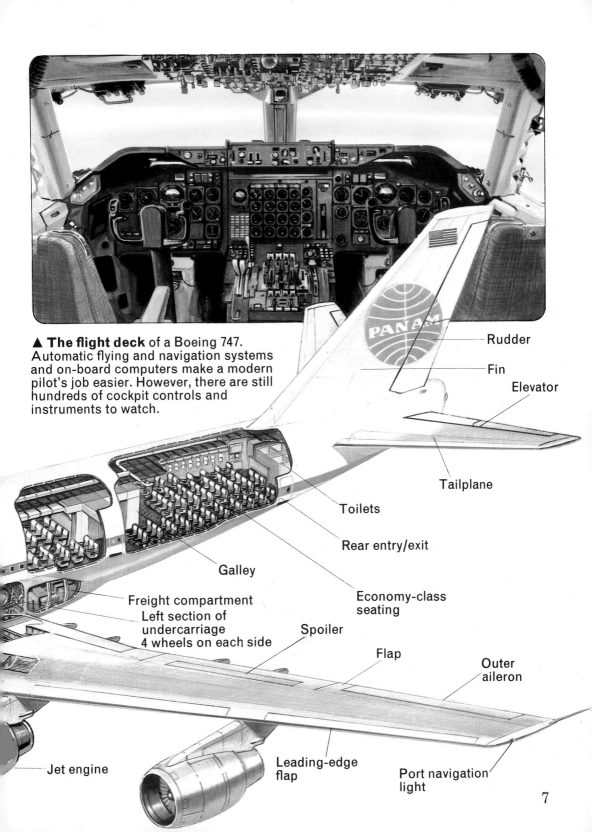

▲ **The flight deck** of a Boeing 747. Automatic flying and navigation systems and on-board computers make a modern pilot's job easier. However, there are still hundreds of cockpit controls and instruments to watch.

Rudder

Fin

Elevator

Tailplane

Toilets

Rear entry/exit

Galley

Economy-class seating

Freight compartment

Left section of undercarriage 4 wheels on each side

Spoiler

Flap

Outer aileron

Jet engine

Leading-edge flap

Port navigation light

Some Early Airliners

The first airliners were simply converted World War I bombers: Farman Goliaths, DH 9s, Vickers Vimys and German LVG CV1s. Aeroplanes had no radios and were navigated by using a map and watching the ground. The passengers, as well as the aircrew, often had to sit in the open.

Then, in the 1920s and early 1930s, airliners and their equipment improved rapidly. Big biplanes like the DH Hercules and HP 42 Hannibal made flying much more comfortable. Top speeds, though, were still under 160 km/h. For really long journeys *flying-boats* still ruled the skies.

All this was to change in 1933 with the Boeing Model 247 which opened the way for fast, reliable, low-fare air travel as we know it.

▲ **Junkers Ju-52/3m** An advanced, three-engined, all metal German monoplane of 1931, seating 15 to 17.

▲ **Farman Goliath** This French aeroplane flew on the first international service in 1919, from Paris to Brussels.

▲ **Vickers Vimy** One of the first airliners; originally a World War I bomber.

▼ **Dornier Do-X** In the 1930s flying-boats were popular on long, over-water routes. This 150-seat, 12-engined German giant was the world's biggest in 1929.

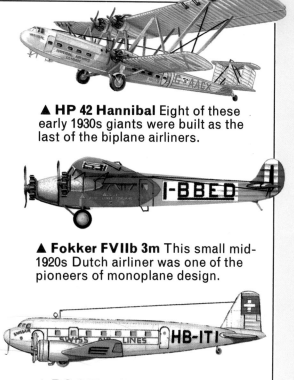

▲ **Blériot-Spad 33** A French airliner typical of the early 1920s. It was slow, small and uncomfortable.

▲ **HP 42 Hannibal** Eight of these early 1930s giants were built as the last of the biplane airliners.

▲ **Ford Tri-motor** The three-engined 'Tin Goose' monoplane of 1926, was popular in the United States.

▲ **Fokker FVIIb 3m** This small mid-1920s Dutch airliner was one of the pioneers of monoplane design.

▲ **DH 86** This 1930s biplane had four engines and could carry up to 16 passengers.

▲ **DC-2** This 1930s airliner had 14 seats and was very advanced for its day.

▲ **DC-3** Over 10,000 Dakotas were built, and many are still in service.

▲ **Vickers Viking** A successful airliner based on the famous Wellington bomber.

▲ **DC-7** Douglas's answer to the Constellation.

◀ **Lockheed Super Constellation** One of the last, and best, of the long-range turboprops.

Propeller-driven Airliners

The world's first jet airliner was the de Havilland Comet 1, which entered service in 1952. However, for many years after propellers were still common on both piston-engined and *turboprop* aircraft.

Until the 1930s, many airliners were simply converted bombers or big biplanes with open flight-decks and a few seats inside.

Then, in 1933, the first really modern, all-metal airliner entered service in America. The Boeing Model 247 (see page 2) was well *streamlined* and had an *automatic pilot* and a retractable undercarriage. It could carry 10 passengers

▼ **Lockheed Electra** The first all-American turboprop; a 645 km/h design from 1959.

▼ **HS 748** A turboprop of the 1960s, it has 58 seats and cruises at 470 km/h.

▼ **NAMC YS-11** Since 1965 over 180 of these 60-seat Japanese aeroplanes have been built.

◀ Boeing Strato-cruiser The first pressurized airliner, built in the early 1950s. Up to 89 passengers could be carried in comfort. It had a small cocktail bar and some sleeping berths (see left).

at a cruising speed of around 250 km/h. But three years later the Douglas DC-3 appeared and soon overshadowed the Model 247. At a speedy 290 km/h the famous 'Dakota' carried 28 to 32 people in comfort. Thousands were built before, during and after World War II, and many are still flying today.

After the War, before the arrival of the new jet aircraft of the late 1950s and early 1960s, prop-driven airliners had one last fling. Powerful new turboprops gave rise to 100-seater giants like the Boeing Stratocruiser, Lockheed Super Constellation, Douglas DC-6 and -7, and the Vickers Vanguard. Cruising along at up to 700 km/h, these high-flying, *pressurized* aeroplanes became the last of a long line of major prop-driven airliners.

▼ Vickers Viscount Perhaps the best medium-range airliner of the 1950s and 1960s.

▼ Fokker Friendship Short on range, but one of the biggest-selling turboprop airliners.

11

Two-engined Jets

Around the world thousands of two-jet airliners are used on short- or medium-distance (240 to 2400 km) routes. They are usually much smaller than three- and four-engined jets, but many two-engined jets fly just as fast.

The first generation of two-jet airliners in the 1950s included the Tu-104 and the Caravelle – the world's first rear-engined jet.

Next came the medium-range DC-9, BAC One-Eleven, Tu-134 and Boeing 737 in the mid-1960s. Since then high-capacity planes like the Mercure and the A300B Airbus have become most popular.

Boeing 737 underside

▼ **Boeing 737** Boeing's commuter airliner of the 1970s, built for short runways and seating 75 to 100.

▼ **Mercure** An advanced, 134-seat, short-haul French airliner of the 1970s.

Airbus A300B underside

▼ **Airbus A300B** Europe's most modern airliner has seats for 345 people on short- and medium-haul routes.

Mercure underside

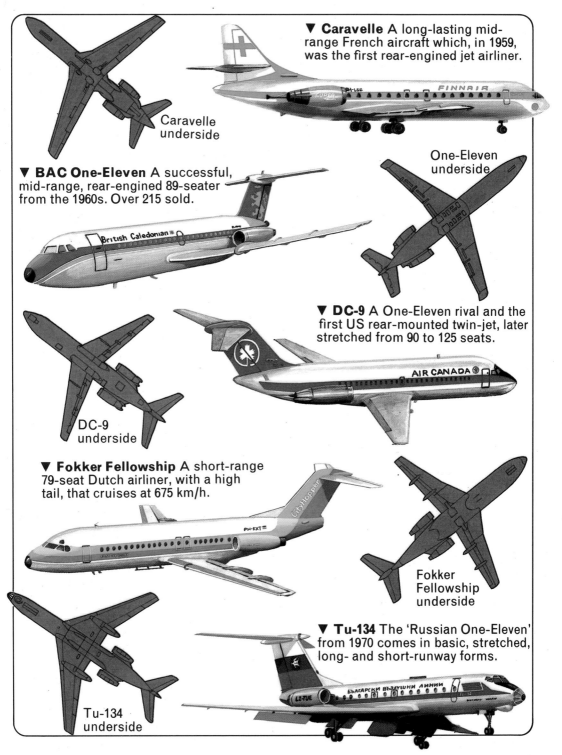

▼ **Caravelle** A long-lasting mid-range French aircraft which, in 1959, was the first rear-engined jet airliner.

Caravelle underside

One-Eleven underside

▼ **BAC One-Eleven** A successful, mid-range, rear-engined 89-seater from the 1960s. Over 215 sold.

▼ **DC-9** A One-Eleven rival and the first US rear-mounted twin-jet, later stretched from 90 to 125 seats.

DC-9 underside

▼ **Fokker Fellowship** A short-range 79-seat Dutch airliner, with a high tail, that cruises at 675 km/h.

Fokker Fellowship underside

▼ **Tu-134** The 'Russian One-Eleven' from 1970 comes in basic, stretched, long- and short-runway forms.

Tu-134 underside

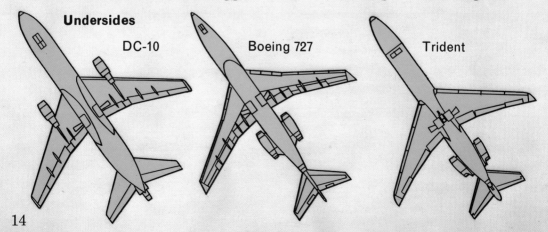

▲ **DC-10** McDonnell Douglas's airbus came out in 1971, and like the TriStar, has been given more powerful engines for long-range flights.

Three-engined Jets

Around the world there was a huge increase in the number of airline passengers during the 1960s. As a result, the size of airliners also had to increase. This was because airports could generally cope with more people, but the skies around them were becoming overcrowded.

So, rather than use small two-jet airliners for short- and medium-distance routes, aircraft designers in the early 1960s decided to make the airliners for these routes bigger.

They could have done this by using four-jet designs, but these are very expensive to run except on inter-continental routes.

Instead, they settled on a three-jet layout, and in 1964 both the Trident and the Boeing 727 entered service. Russia's Tu-154 – the 'Tupolev Trident' – followed in 1971. Meanwhile, powerful new *turbofan* engines have produced the 400-seat TriStar and the DC-10 wide-bodied 'airbuses'. Both of these designs are being *stretched* for use on long-distance flights.

Undersides

DC-10   Boeing 727   Trident

▲ **Boeing 727** Boeing's 1964 tri-jet uses many of the same fuselage parts as the 707, and has been stretched to give a 3000-kilometre range.

▲ **Hawker Siddeley Trident** At 1000 km/h, with a 1600-kilometre range and 100 to 150 seats, this rear-engined tri-jet followed the Comet in 1964.

▲ **TriStar** In 1972 the wide-bodied Lockheed L-1011 became the second US airbus. It has also been stretched to a long-haul 400-seater.

▲ **Tu-154** The 'Tupolev Trident' can take off in 1140 metres, and has been stretched from 158 to 240 seats.

TriStar

Tu-154

Four-engined Jets

Big, intercontinental, four-engined airliners have always been symbols of airline comfort, speed and style.

Once, the 95-seat Super Constellation, with its 523 km/h cruising speed and 4400-kilometre range, was thought impressive. Nowadays, less than 25 years on, Boeing 747s, with up to 490 seats, regularly fly at around 950 km/h on journeys up to 9000 kilometres. Even the 189-seat 707 (introduced as the first four-jet airliner in 1958) cruises at around 950 km/h for almost eight hours. The future promises even bigger and faster 'superjets'.

Boeing 747
underside

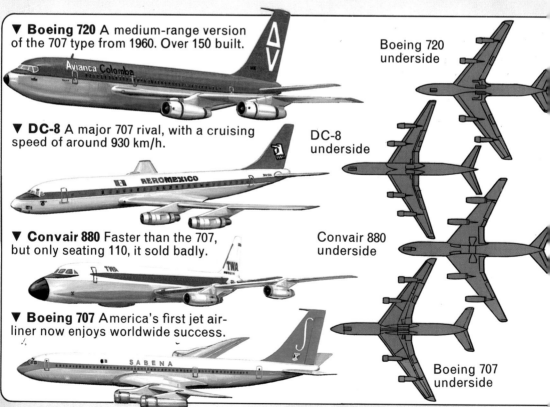

▼ **Boeing 720** A medium-range version of the 707 type from 1960. Over 150 built.

Boeing 720
underside

▼ **DC-8** A major 707 rival, with a cruising speed of around 930 km/h.

DC-8
underside

▼ **Convair 880** Faster than the 707, but only seating 110, it sold badly.

Convair 880
underside

▼ **Boeing 707** America's first jet airliner now enjoys worldwide success.

Boeing 707
underside

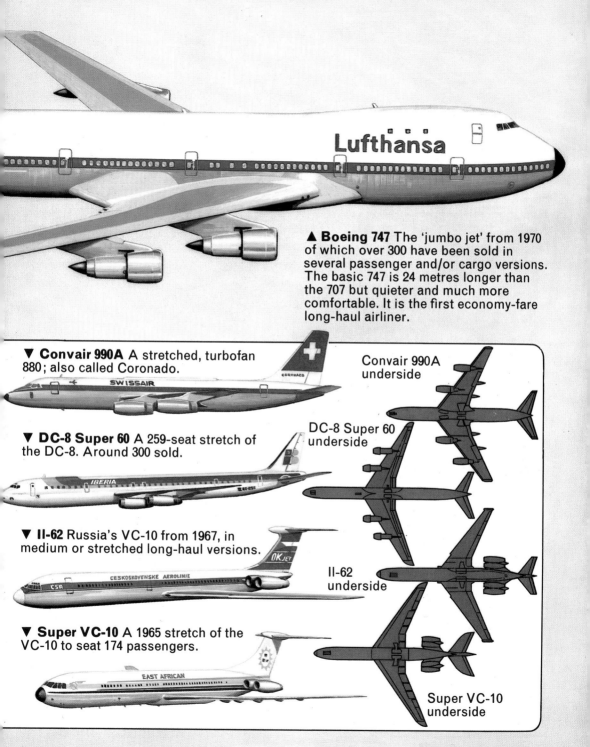

▲ Boeing 747 The 'jumbo jet' from 1970 of which over 300 have been sold in several passenger and/or cargo versions. The basic 747 is 24 metres longer than the 707 but quieter and much more comfortable. It is the first economy-fare long-haul airliner.

▼ Convair 990A A stretched, turbofan 880; also called Coronado.

SWISSAIR

Convair 990A underside

▼ DC-8 Super 60 A 259-seat stretch of the DC-8. Around 300 sold.

IBERIA

DC-8 Super 60 underside

▼ Il-62 Russia's VC-10 from 1967, in medium or stretched long-haul versions.

CESKOSLOVENSKE AEROLINIE

CSA

OK JET

Il-62 underside

▼ Super VC-10 A 1965 stretch of the VC-10 to seat 174 passengers.

EAST AFRICAN

Super VC-10 underside

Supersonic Airliners

▲ **Concorde** with its slim delta-wing shape is ideal for supersonic flight. It carries up to 140 passengers.

Aircraft that can travel faster than the speed at which sound moves through the air are called 'supersonic'. In order to do this they must pass through the shock waves of the so-called sound barrier. Above 11,000 metres, where supersonic aeroplanes can cruise, the air is cold and 'thin', and the sound barrier is at around 1060 km/h. If the aircraft is well designed to withstand them, these shock waves present no problems. Otherwise, it is likely to be shaken to pieces very quickly. As a result, both the world's supersonic airliners – Concorde and the Tu-144 – are masterpieces of *aerodynamic* design, using the best materials available.

They both have delta wings, as a dart-like shape is best for very high-speed control. They can also cruise at over 2000 km/h for almost three hours. Unfortunately, supersonic travel is expensive, and may be a luxury for years to come.

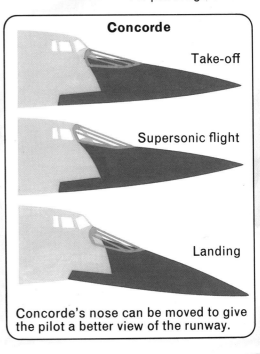

Concorde

Take-off

Supersonic flight

Landing

Concorde's nose can be moved to give the pilot a better view of the runway.

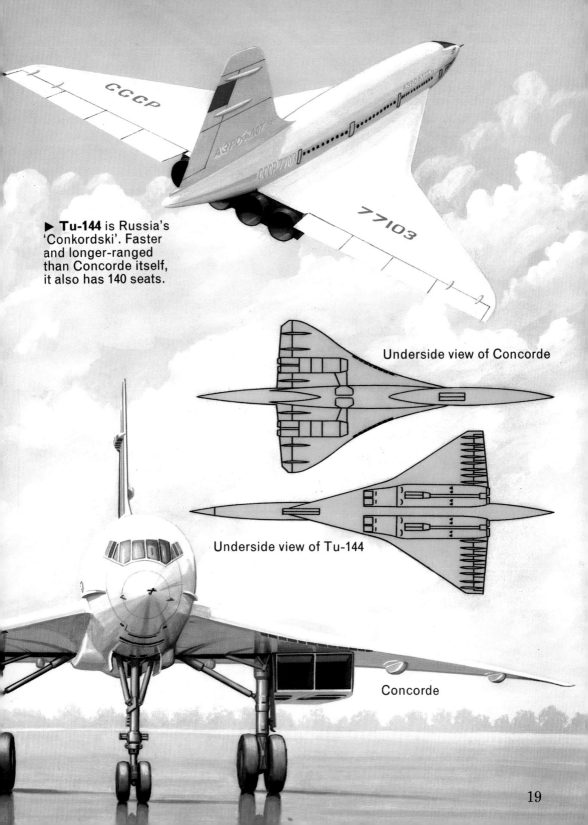

▶ **Tu-144** is Russia's 'Conkordski'. Faster and longer-ranged than Concorde itself, it also has 140 seats.

Underside view of Concorde

Underside view of Tu-144

Concorde

19

Airline Insignia

Studying the badges on aeroplanes will help you to identify different airlines. But do not be surprised if these insignia vary from time to time, or from aeroplane to aeroplane.

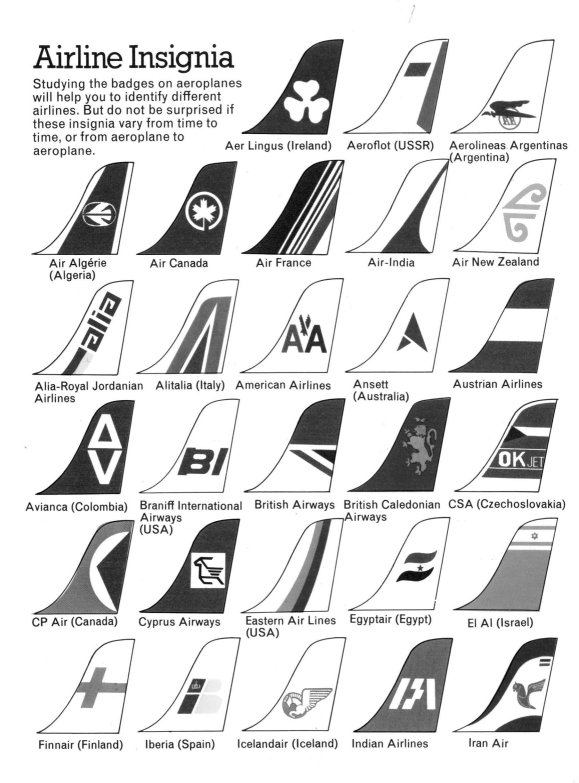

Aer Lingus (Ireland)

Aeroflot (USSR)

Aerolineas Argentinas (Argentina)

Air Algérie (Algeria)

Air Canada

Air France

Air-India

Air New Zealand

Alia-Royal Jordanian Airlines

Alitalia (Italy)

American Airlines

Ansett (Australia)

Austrian Airlines

Avianca (Colombia)

Braniff International Airways (USA)

British Airways

British Caledonian Airways

CSA (Czechoslovakia)

CP Air (Canada)

Cyprus Airways

Eastern Air Lines (USA)

Egyptair (Egypt)

El Al (Israel)

Finnair (Finland)

Iberia (Spain)

Icelandair (Iceland)

Indian Airlines

Iran Air

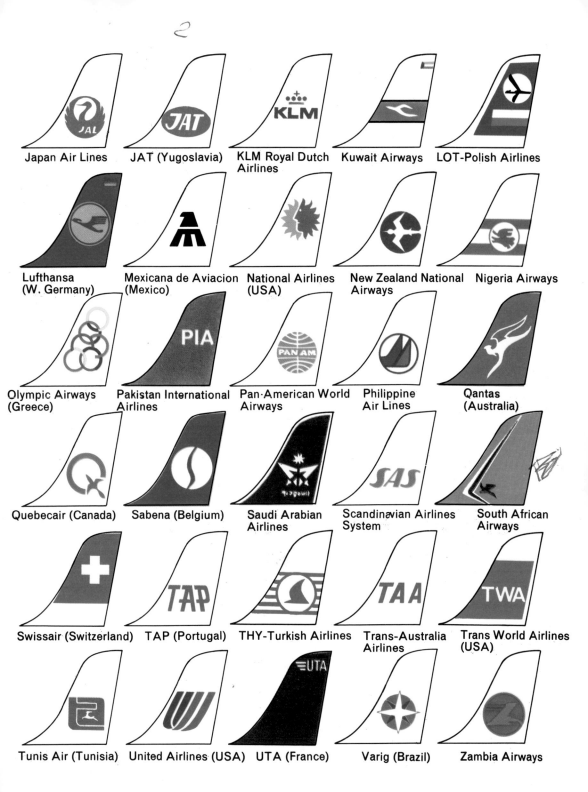

Japan Air Lines JAT (Yugoslavia) KLM Royal Dutch Airlines Kuwait Airways LOT-Polish Airlines

Lufthansa (W. Germany) Mexicana de Aviacion (Mexico) National Airlines (USA) New Zealand National Airways Nigeria Airways

Olympic Airways (Greece) Pakistan International Airlines Pan-American World Airways Philippine Air Lines Qantas (Australia)

Quebecair (Canada) Sabena (Belgium) Saudi Arabian Airlines Scandinavian Airlines System South African Airways

Swissair (Switzerland) TAP (Portugal) THY-Turkish Airlines Trans-Australia Airlines Trans World Airlines (USA)

Tunis Air (Tunisia) United Airlines (USA) UTA (France) Varig (Brazil) Zambia Airways

At an Airport

The control tower and its computers are the heart of any airport. From there, all aircraft movements in, out and on the ground are watched on radar and directed by radio. Aircraft also need maintenance and fuel, and cargo has to be handled and stored. Last – but not least – there are the passengers, needing everything from car parks and food to emergency doctors. With problems of noise pollution as well, running a busy modern airport is a very complicated business.

The World's Busiest Airports

Chicago International Airport in the USA is the world's busiest commercial airport. It not only handles international flights, but also many other services to and from other American cities. Each year around 40 million passengers pass through, and there are about 750,000 aircraft movements. This means an aircraft lands or takes-off *every* 45 seconds, night and day!

Many other airports, like Frankfurt, Amsterdam's Schiphol, London's Heathrow and New York's Kennedy, are also very busy. They have planes coming in or leaving almost every minute.

Dallas-Fort Worth Airport in Texas, USA, will have nine runways and 13 terminals when it is finished. It will then be the world's biggest, able to handle 60 million people a year.

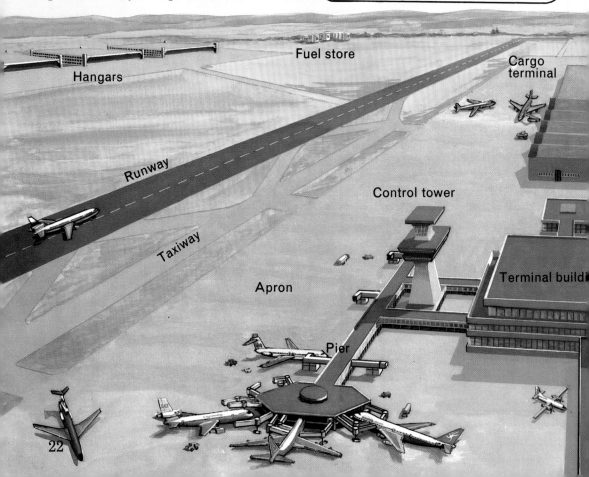

Hangars

Fuel store

Cargo terminal

Runway

Control tower

Taxiway

Apron

Terminal buildi

Pier

Glossary

Aerodynamics The study of the way in which air moves around a flying object such as an aircraft.

Airship A gas-filled balloon with a frame, engines and passenger cabins. These aircraft were popular for long-distance journeys in the 1920s and 1930s.

Automatic pilot A remote control system which can be used to let the aeroplane fly itself on a particular course.

Biplane An aircraft with two sets of wings, one above the other.

Flying-boat An aircraft with a boat-like hull that lands and takes off from water.

Fuselage The body of an aeroplane.

Monoplane An aircraft with one set of wings.

Pressurization Keeping air pressure inside an aircraft artificially normal. This is done so that aircraft can fly high and therefore burn less fuel. The occupants can still breathe even though the outside air is too 'thin' to maintain life.

Prototype The first aeroplane built to a new design. It is usually used for testing.

Streamlining Designing an aircraft or its parts to put up the least resistance to the air when in flight. It has been an important feature of modern airliners since the Boeing Model 247 appeared in 1933.

Stretch An aircraft is 'stretched' by adding new sections to make the *fuselage* longer. Usually, new 'stretched' aeroplanes are built, rather than old aeroplanes converted.

Turbine A machine which works by the rapid turning of bladed discs.

Turbofan A *turbojet* engine with a big extra fan to draw in more air and so increase the power of the engine.

Turbojet An engine that uses *turbines* to squeeze air, explode it, and force the exhaust out in a jet to power the forward movement of an aircraft.

Turboprop A jet engine that drives a propeller.

Index

Books to Read

Airliners since 1946 by Kenneth Munson (Blandford Press)

Airliners between the Wars by Kenneth Munson (Blandford Press)

Aircraft by B. Williams (Sampson Low)

Aircraft by John W. R. Taylor (Hamlyn)

See Inside an Airport by Jonathan Rutland (Hutchinson)

The World's Airports by John Stroud (Bodley Head)

Airports in Action by T. Burret and B. Kemp (Ward Lock)

Airports by C. King (Blackie)